PRIORITY TO PURSUE

Things That Matter - Living A Life Of Purpose

Enriqueta R. Holder

Copyright © by [Enriqueta R. Holder] 2022

The author reserves all rights. Except for brief quotations incorporated in critical reviews and certain other noncommercial uses permitted by copyright law, no part of this publication may be reproduced, distributed, or transmitted in any form or by any means, including photocopying, recording, or other electronic or mechanical methods, without the publisher's prior written permission.

Table Of Content

INTRODUCTION

CHAPTER ONE - Master your internal triggers

CHAPTER TWO - Discover What Holds You Back

CHAPTER THREE - Create your vision and let clarity guide you.

CHAPTER FOUR - Prioritize Time

CHAPTER FIVE - Dealing with distractions

CHAPTER SIX - No Rush - Slowing Down

INTRODUCTION

Today's society has far too much to accomplish and far too little leisure. Your jobs, tasks, and responsibilities frequently overwhelm you. The goal for you is to simplify your life so that you can spend more time on the things that matter most to you and less time on the ones that don't.

The good news is that you have the ability to live a life without regrets right now, in which you are completely engaged in your relationships and all you do. You can choose to live a life that gives meaning and purpose to each day and brings you delight. You can live a life that is focused, positive, and in perfect harmony with the person you are deep inside.

Your happiness and well-being are based on your desire for peace of mind and the concept of having a balanced existence. You will enjoy the happiness you deserve and experience harmony among all the aspects that make up a successful life for you, as you define it, when you begin to live your life in balance as the greatest person you can possibly be..

It takes life control to be capable of accomplishing what you set out to do. People who have effective life control are skilled at planning and time management, and they are at ease with accomplishing multiple tasks at once.

They have the ability to recognize that they may not have the time to accomplish a task right away and will schedule it for later. Avoiding distractions is an important component of controlling your time's efficacy.

Distraction?

Distraction is the process of diverting an individual's or a group's attention away from a desired area of focus, preventing or reducing the reception of desired information. Distraction is caused by: the lack of ability to pay attention; lack of interest in the object of attention; or the great intensity, novelty or attractiveness of something other than the object of attention. Distractions come from both external sources, and internal sources. External distractions include factors such as visual triggers, social interactions, music, text messages, and phone calls. There are also internal distractions such as hunger, fatigue, illness, worrying, and daydreaming. Both external and internal distractions contribute to the interference of focus.

For example, Co-workers dropping by to ask a question is a common workplace distraction. So much that employees usually spend about 11 minutes focused on a project in one go before being interrupted. They'll require roughly 25 minutes to refocus on the project task at hand after that.

Distraction, in the context of fiction, is an escape from unpleasantness. It's a convenient way to avoid inconvenience.

We synthesize the insights that will allow you to efficiently prioritize your time and conquer distractions in this book.

CHAPTER ONE

Master your internal triggers

"The majority of diversions originate within us, and we utilize distraction to avoid suffering." Nir Eyal (Nir Eyal)

It's past time to put the blame on technology.

Yes, there are external triggers that cause you to become distracted, but according to Eyal, the most prevalent cause of distraction is internal triggers, or the unpleasant sensations we want to avoid. These triggers cause you to engage in distracted behaviors that place you in a different mental state.

You'll always be able to find anything to distract yourself from the internal emotion you're trying to avoid. To eliminate the psychological need for this diversion, you must first identify the feelings (internal triggers) that cause you to seek it in the first place.

Nature has placed humans under the rule of two sovereign rulers, according to Jeremy Bentham: pain and pleasure. The desire to be free of discomfort, on the other hand, is the driving force behind all of our actions.

As a result, in order to master distraction, we must first master discomfort management. People often stay helpless victims in a tragedy of their own making without strategies to comprehend and skillfully address this process.

Master your internal triggers so that they lead you to the tasks you want to perform rather than the ones you'd rather avoid. It all starts with acknowledgment. You can't change what you're not aware of.

Begin to notice your diversions and the emotions you experience when you enter them. Do you use Facebook or Instagram to connect with others when you're lonely? Do you find yourself surfing around Reddit or watching the news when you're bored? Do you pull out your phone and check email to appear "busy" when you're self-conscious in public, or do you get a drink to keep yourself occupied?

We live in a world where people are desperately trying to get away from themselves.

Diversions can even be mistaken for constructive behaviors, when they are actually distractions hiding behind a mask. Ask yourself this question: do you utilize meditation to avoid taking action? Do you use the gym as an excuse to avoid performing the work you know you should be doing?

When you understand your own triggers, you can finally allow yourself to experience the emotion you've been avoiding or running away from. Take a moment the next time you're uncomfortable and grab for your phone to halt and feel the discomfort. Instead of seeing this as a flaw, take pleasure in the fact that you were able to push through the discomfort and see it as an opportunity for progress rather than a sign of weakness.

As a human species, success implies always wanting more, and the only way to get there is to push your boundaries, including your emotional boundaries.

According to Eyal and Li, how we respond to unpleasant internal cues affects whether we pursue healthy traction or self-defeating

distractions. They state:

Learn to identify and understand the root cause of your internal distraction. All motivation stems from a desire to avoid discomfort, and anything that alleviates discomfort has the potential to be addictive. If you can identify and get to know the drivers of your behavior, you can better manage it.

If distraction costs us time, then effective time management is pain management, according to Eyal and Li. They recognize the necessity of leveraging dissatisfaction's power. This is based on dispelling the myth that if we aren't joyful, we aren't normal.

4 steps to assist us deal with distracting (invasive) thoughts;

Step 1: Pay attention to the discomfort that occurs before distractions: concentrate on the internal cause (feeling anxious, having a craving, feeling restless, or feeling you are incompetent).

Step 2: Make a list of the internal triggers: (time, what you were doing, how you felt). We will be able to manage the behavior better over time if you are better at spotting it.

Step 3: When you're about to be distracted, pay attention to your sensations (fingers twitching, butterflies in your tummy).

Imagine yourself seated alongside a softly running stream, according to Bricker's technique for effectively responding to and coping with internal, distracting sensations. Imagine a stream of leaves slowly pouring down it. Put each of your emotions/thoughts on a leaf. Simply sit back and let the leaves float down the stream. You will be able to control these sensations as a result of this (internal triggers).

Step 4: Keep an eye out for liminal periods (transitional moments in your day) These are the times when you're prone to becoming distracted.

"The Ten-Minute Rule" — If you're tempted to do anything distracting (check your phone, watch another episode of Netflix), tell yourself not to give in right away. Allow yourself ten minutes before deciding whether or not to continue with the distracting behavior.

CHAPTER TWO

Find out what's holding you back.

You can tell when you are living in accordance with your principles because you have peace of mind, tranquillity, and even joy. You feel the opposite when you are off balance and off track. Nature's way of telling you to return to your ideals is through negative emotions, dissatisfaction, and discontent of any type. Returning to what is truly essential to you and then refusing to compromise your principles will almost instantly restore your sense of calm and pleasure.

Everyone has been in a difficult position, an uncomfortable relationship, or a lousy job at some point in their lives. As the situation worsened, you felt compelled to compromise your principles rather than doing what you knew was right and insisting on your own happiness and well-being. You became more worried, miserable, and detached from life and other people the longer you were in that horrible environment.

Finally, you inhaled deeply, summoned your bravery, and resolved to "do the right thing." Even though you didn't know what you were

going to do and had debts to pay, you walked away from the awful employment. Even though you had no idea how you'd ever find another, better relationship, you moved away from the poor one.

Then something incredible occurred! You were giddy with delight. You were in a fantastic state. You were relieved and thrilled. IIt felt as if a massive burden had been lifted from your shoulders. As you walked away, you were overjoyed and nearly laughed out loud.

What was the reasoning behind it? Simple is the answer. Nature rewards you by giving you a feeling of joy and contentment whenever you decide to return to your values and get back on track. This happy emotion is intended to motivate you to conduct your life more consistently in accordance with your ideals.

Happiness' Obstacles

Your values are undeniably important in your life and everything that occurs to you. For success, self-esteem, pleasure, and peace of mind, it's critical to live by your values. When you go against or compromise your essential ideas and values, you feel uneasy, unhappy, agitated, and anxious, and your self-esteem suffers. You don't like or respect yourself as much as you used to. This is why

we believe that returning to your beliefs can fix practically any problem in your personal life.

Prioritize your own happiness.

Those who plainly and distinctively exhibit their own unique personalities are the most admired persons in every culture. They are adamant and unwavering in their ideals and views, refusing to compromise them for anybody or anything.

Ayn Rand was famous for stating that your biggest value or purpose in life should be achieving your own happiness. She claims that how joyful you feel about yourself minute by minute and hour by hour can tell you how successful you are. Your own happiness should be the yardstick by which you measure your activities, behaviors, and most importantly, values.

On this subject, there is some ambiguity. People are taught that finding happiness for oneself is in some way selfish. We are meant to put others' happiness first. But the reality is that you can't give away what you don't have. You can't make someone else happy unless you're satisfied with your own happiness. Become a truly happy person if you truly want to make others

happy. There isn't any other option.

You work from your equilibrium point when you are clear about your values, goals, and priorities. You'll feel cheerful, clear, and concentrated as a result. You face each day with boldness and assurance.

Balance, Authenticity, and Values

At the very least, you must choose to be honest to one person: yourself. The only way to succeed at establishing and working from your balancing point is to have integrity and authenticity. "To thine own self be true, and it must follow, as the night the day, thou canst not then be untrue to any man," Shakespeare wrote.

Keep in mind that your balancing point is unique to you. You may discover that you share values with others and that you can connect and relate to them based on those principles, but you will also discover that you have a lot of differences. Your objective is to figure out what's right for you and then have the fortitude and confidence to live your own set of principles for the rest of your life.

Don't let comparisons to others make you feel intimidated or cause you to question your ideals. You must do what is best for you while also accepting that others are doing what is best for them.

There are three sets of values.

Consider a group of three women. The first woman decided soon after graduation that she wanted to marry and start a family. She decided to pursue her job once her children had graduated from high school. The second woman opted to pursue a job after college and worked hard for ten years to establish a strong reputation and achieve success in her chosen field. It was only then that she decided to start a family. The third lady chose to do both: advance her career while simultaneously marrying and raising a family. Although all three women shared the principles of having a profession and being a mother, they each went about achieving those goals in their own way. Each of the three approaches was a representation of one woman's ideals and unique equilibrium point.

Make the decision to live a beautiful life today. Examine each of the hurdles to happiness—the justifications people use for abandoning their true ideals and settling for less than their true

potential.

Keep in mind that each of these roadblocks exists only in your head, in your thoughts. You can let go of your self-limiting beliefs at any time and become a fully functioning, fully developed, and fully happy person. You have the ability to break free from your limits and fulfill your full potential. You can choose your own equilibrium point, your own set of values and objectives, and return to it at any time.

CHAPTER THREE

Create your vision and let clarity guide you.

As you begin your quest for a purposeful existence, your capacity to construct a clear, thrilling picture of your ideal life at some point in the future is your beginning point. The target you're aiming towards is your ideal life vision. You must focus all of your efforts, time, and energy on that aim in order to feel involved and present every day. To put it another way, if you want to achieve your personal and professional goals while maintaining genuine balance, you must be clear about what you want to achieve.

Consider the possibility of having no restrictions.

Begin by assuming that you are completely free of all constraints. Imagine being able to be, do, or have anything you choose in the world.

What you truly, really, really want to do with your life is the main question.

Consider having a magic wand with which you could wave over any aspect of your life and make it perfect in every way. What would be different from how things are now?

Your perceptions become your reality.

Perhaps the most important finding in human history is that you are most often what you think about.

What do you ponder the majority of the time? "Your outer world will tend to be a reflection of your inner world," says the Law of Correspondence. This concept is true in a wide range of situations, from the things you want to obtain or attain to your core ideas about yourself and others.

Your reticular activating system is triggered by what you think about most of the time, causing you to become more aware of items in your environment. If you decide to acquire a red car, for example, you will begin to notice red cars everywhere. People around you will appear pleasant and well-natured if you feel people are generally kind with good intentions.

It's a two-way street.

Unfortunately, your thoughts are a double-edged blade. If you feel that people are untrustworthy and hostile, you will see examples of this all around you. Your views and how you see the world on the inside will have a direct impact on how you experience the world outside yourself. "You don't believe what you see; you see what you already believe," as the saying goes. What you believe is a reflection of who you are, of your deepest beliefs about yourself and the world.

Everything you see outside of you mirrors something that is going on inside of you, something that is important to you. To live an outstanding life, you must create a detailed, vivid picture of what your ideal life might look like. Once you've decided what you want, the universe's enormous power will begin to manifest it in the world around you. You'll begin to attract the people and resources you need to make your ambitions a reality. Opportunities will start to present themselves to assist you in achieving your ideal life, just as you have imagined it.

This isn't to say that if you visualize your ideal life, it would arrive without any work on your part. However, you can only start living your ideal life once you've decided what it looks like. It's impossible to hit a target that you can't see.

Always keep in mind that life is a journey. It is up to you to decide what type of trip you will take. You are allowed to imagine your ideal life destination and then figure out how to get there.

The Magic Question

Can you guess what happy, successful people spend the most of their time thinking about? The answer is both straightforward and astounding. Most of the time, top people are thinking about what they want and how to obtain it. They spend the most of their time thinking about achieving and enjoying their goals, objectives, and ambitions. They are continually inquiring as to how the magic works.

How does the leader, the optimist, the builder, the mover and shaker answer this question? When you ask how, you're eliciting ideas for activities you can take to advance faster in your life in all areas.

The top 10% of people spend the majority of their time thinking about the future. They spend the majority of their time thinking about where they're going and what they desire. They face a variety of challenges and boldly find their way around them. They consider the daily measures they might take to draw themselves closer to their hopes and dreams. They merely want to know how.

Develop your leadership skills.

You are in charge of your own life. You are in charge of your own destiny. This is something only you can do; no one else can.

Future-oriented persons are characterized by their constant idealization of their lives and their future. They see themselves in the future and imagine it to be wonderful in every way. They then return to the present and choose what they must do, beginning now, in order to build the future they wish. This is something you can do, too.

To begin, you must gain clarity in four essential areas: who you are, what matters most to you, and what you want to do in the future.

Area 1: Creating Your Professional Identity—Building Your Business

Area 2: Your Personal and Family Relationships

Area 3: Your Personal Health

Area 4: Your Financial Assets and Investments

CHAPTER FOUR

Prioritize Time

How to Prioritize Daily Tasks to Manage Time

Time management success hinges on the ability to prioritize everyday responsibilities. Prioritizing ensures that the most critical tasks are completed first. Make time management a habit - you'll thank yourself (and your boss!) later. Follow the steps below:

Begin by making a master list.

Make a list of all the tasks you need to complete, both routine and vital. At this time, there is no need to rank the objects.

Make careful to incorporate normal responsibilities. Your well-intentioned time-block schedule can be thrown off if you forget to schedule the mundane must-do tasks.

Determine the top priority A-level tasks – those that, if not completed today, will have serious effects.

Focusing on the repercussions provides a sense of urgency, which allows you to make better use of your time. If you have a scheduled presentation today, that activity will undoubtedly be at the top of your priority list.

Sort the remaining tasks into categories. Use the following categories:

B-level tasks: Activities that, if not accomplished today, may have a little negative impact.

C-level chores *are those that don't have any consequences if they aren't finished today.*

D-level tasks: *The letter D stands for delegate. These are actions that can be carried out by someone else.*

Tasks on the E-level: *Tasks that could be removed. Make no attempt to write an E next to them; simply cross them out.*

Within each category, rank the tasks.

If you have six A, four B, three C, and two D things on your list, Your six A jobs naturally rise to the top of the list, but you must now prioritize these six items in the following order: A-1, A-2, A-3, and so on.

So, what about the D's? They're ready to be handed off to someone else! Consider the rule of 85/10/5: You spend 85 percent of your time doing chores that anyone else could do, 10% of your time doing actions that some others could handle, and only 5% of your time doing work that only you can do. Concentrate on the crucial 5% and identify the remaining chores that are the easiest to delegate.

Every day, repeat the process.

Some Bs will be promoted, while others will remain in the B category. Some Cs may overtake the Bs to become the highest priority As.

What are your time-management strategies? 24 Time Prioritization Tips

1. Make a list of goals and stick to them.

Goals are similar to a road map. They give us a starting point as well as step-by-step directions to our target. They do, however, help us stay focused. If you've ever driven in new country, you'll know how important it is to keep your eyes on the road so you don't miss a turn.

Prior to accomplishing anything else, make a list of your objectives and stick to them.

Run a SWOT analysis. Short for strengths, weaknesses, opportunities, and threats, this is where you identify the challenges in these four areas. Knowing this, you can then look for ways to overcomes these obstacles.

2. Make a master list of every item you want to include.

Those objectives you just devised? Add them to a to-do list, along with any other projects, meetings, or domestic duties that need to be completed. The order isn't important right now. All you have to

do now is get these ideas out of your head and into a notebook or piece of paper. You might also use Evernote, Google Keep, or Todoist as digital tools.

Some of you may end up with a long and daunting list as a result of this. Don't worry about it. Go over your to-do list and start cutting the fat by organizing it by date-specific duties. Deadlines, due dates, and events previously scheduled on your calendar are all examples. Also, concentrate exclusively on the most crucial tasks that require your immediate attention.

What about the remainder of your to-do list? If there is something you need to do but it isn't urgent, put it on your to-do list. Assign items that can be delegated or outsourced to someone else if they can be. And, if there's anything on your list that isn't a good use of your time, cross it off.

3. Develop a fondness for Ike.

Even if your to-do list isn't as long as mine, prioritizing it can be difficult. Using a priority matrix, such as the iconic Eisenhower Matrix, is one technique to apply here.

Here's what you need to know if you're not a history buff. Dwight Eisenhower, also known as Ike, was given the name Eisenhower Matrix. During World War II, he was the 34th President of the United States and the supreme commander of the Allied Forces in Europe. So, yes, he needed to put his time to good use. And he did so by categorizing all of his tasks into four quadrants:

Important and Urgent — tasks that must be completed as soon as possible.

Not urgent and vital — actions that need to be attended to, but not right now.

Not important or time-sensitive — responsibilities that can be delegated to someone else so that they do not divert your attention.

Time-wasters that should be removed totally from your to-do list because they are neither important nor urgent.

4. Apply to MIT.

Not in the literal sense. Congratulations, however, if you have applied to and been admitted to the Massachusetts Institute of Technology.

The MIT I'm referring to is the most crucial task you have. Without a doubt, it's the one thing you want or need to get done today. It should always be in line with the objectives you've established for yourself.

5. It's as simple as A, B, and C.

Another method for prioritizing your time is to adopt a system that categorizes everything into A, B, and C categories. Here's how it works, according to Steve Tobak:

A stands for important things. These are the items that must be completed immediately or face consequences.

B stands for "business as usual." Everything you need to concentrate on in order to meet your short- and long-term objectives.

C stands for "everything else." Items such as busy work that would be nice to get to or just goofing around fall under this category.

According to Tobak, the beauty of this method is that you'll "really never get to the Priority C jobs." In fact, because anything that doesn't play a substantial role in helping you reach your goals is relegated to the C list, this method drives you to be very specific on your goals."

6. Tidy up your to-do lists with KonMari.

I'm sure you've heard of Marie Kondo's decluttering method: does this bring you joy? If it isn't, then toss it out or donate it. But how does this apply to time management?

We often over-commit ourselves due to FOMO and a fear of saying "no." We also feel compelled to cram as much as possible into each day so that you may portray us as industrious. In actuality, the more we add to our to-do list, the slower we'll make progress. What is the explanation for this? We're more concerned with how much we get done each day than with spending time on the appropriate things.

This can be aided by decluttering your life. It reduces stress, helps you to make fewer decisions, and encourages you to spend more time on the things that are actually important to you.

Amy Jen Su suggests on HBR that you can do this by filtering your priorities. "Select a couple of areas to set priorities in; this can help the brain to manage information overload," explains Amy.

"Researchers have found that it's the overload of options that paralyze us or lead to decisions that go against our best interests," she adds. "Two criteria I use with clients to filter for priorities include contribution and passion." Your highest contribution would be things your purpose, strengths, and experience. Your passion would be the things that motivate and excite you.

7. Follow the 1-3-5 scheduling rule.

Remember that master you created? Go back and use that to shape your day using the 1-3-5 scheduling rule.

Choose the highest priority for today from the list. Nothing else matters in this situation. This is your main objective for the day.

Decide on three medium-term goals. These should ideally be subtasks related to your top priority.

Also, put no more than five tiny must-dos, such as meetings, in your calendar. While these are essential and deserving of your attention, we refer to them as minor to-dos because they demand less effort.

8. Make use of the weighing scales method.

Leon Ho, the creator and CEO of Lifehack, invented the scales approach. You're categorizing your to-do list by importance and the rewards you'll obtain, similar to a priority matrix.

However, in this case, you would prioritize each of your jobs by:

Low-cost + high-reward. These are simple activities to do, but they will help you get closer to your objectives.

The cost is high, but the benefit is high. Large work would be broken down into smaller, more manageable chunks here.

Low-cost and low-benefit options are available. These are the tasks that are least important to you, such as checking your inbox.

Low benefit at a high cost. Time wasters that could be automated or delegated would be found here.

9. Determine your 20%.

Vilfredo Pareto, an Italian economist and sociologist, devised the 80/20 rule, which is also known as the Pareto Principle. This guideline "clearly implies that 80 percent of your results come from 20 percent of your efforts," as Choncé Maddox explains for Calendar.

How does this assist you in prioritizing your tasks? "If you've discovered that 20% of your effort yields 80% of your results," Choncé says, "you'll want to prioritize and increase that 20% margin."

Keeping this in mind, you should always prioritize your 20 percent. If you're having trouble with this, ask yourself, "Are there any duties that, no matter what else happens during the day, would make you feel relieved if you completed them?"

10. Use the 18-minute method.

18 Minutes: A Novel by Peter Bregman This strategy is based on the book Find Your Focus, Master Distraction, and Get the Job Done. In actuality, it's a daily practice that will help you stay focused on your goals throughout the day.

Step 1: Before you do anything else, take five minutes to plan out your day.

Step 2: Check in for a minute every hour to assist you get back on track.

Step 3: At the end of the day, take five minutes to reflect on what went well and what went wrong. Remember to keep track of when you were the most focused.

11. Pay attention to the oracle.

I'm referring to Warren Buffett, called the Oracle of Omaha. It's not about how to invest your money, either. Rather, it's about how you should use your time. Begin by listing your top 25 objectives. After that, draw a circle around the five you believe are the most crucial. What about the other 20 objectives you mentioned? Avoid them at all costs so that you may focus entirely on your top 5.

12. Keep track of due dates and deadlines.

Is this self-evident? Absolutely. However, many people have a habit of biting off more than they can chew. For instance, you may have had a conference call scheduled for months at 4 p.m. on Tuesday. You squeeze in one final job before the call in order to remain ahead of your workload. It's 4:05 before you realize it. That's not cool.

Adding buffers between tasks and events is another example. Assume you have two meetings scheduled for the afternoon. The first is at 2 p.m., while the second is at 3 p.m. At 2:50 p.m., the first meeting, which is across town, concludes. You're not going to be able to make it to the other meeting on time. That's why, to account for the commute, you should leave a buffer between these events.

In other words, if you have something on your calendar already, whether it's a deadline or an appointment, your day should revolve around that entry. It was the first to arrive. It's also simply plain impolite.

13. The best policy is honesty.

I understand. As cliche as peanut butter and jelly, that saying is true. Assume you've planned two meetings for the afternoon. The first will begin at 2:00 p.m., while the second will begin at 3:00 p.m. The first meeting, which is across town, ends at 2:50 p.m. You won't be able to make it to the second meeting on time. As a result, you should leave a delay between these events to accommodate for the commute.

To put it another way, if you already have something in your schedule, whether it's a deadline or an appointment, your day should revolve around it. It was the very first to show up. It's also considered impolite.

13. Honesty is the best policy.

I see your point. That cliche is as accurate as peanut butter and jelly.

14. Make every day count.

I'm not trying to be all new-agey on you. But, personally, that should be a top priority for everyone. Of course, that doesn't mean living recklessly. It's all about spending your time wisely. If that

means leaving work early to spend time with your fam, then so be it. If that's preparing to meet with investors in order to secure a much-need loan for your business, then it's all good.

If you want to know how this is done, I recommend you check out Benjamin Franklin's daily schedule. It's simple while providing structure. And, most importantly, it forces you to answer, "What good shall I do this day?"

15. Do what you dread first.

At some point, you've probably had to move. Even if you haven't, you've aided a friend or family member in some way. Unless, of course, you've always had someone do it for you. And if that's the case, I'm quite envious.

Anyway, let's not waste any more time. Moving is a drag. It's both mentally and physically draining. When I have to make the dreaded move, though, I always begin with the heaviest stuff. There are two reasons for this.

For one thing, after a long day of moving, do you really want to move a bedroom dresser? Obviously not. You're tired and ready for the day to be over. Second, removing the bigger and heavier components makes everything else seem to run more smoothly. I suppose it's because now that the big thing is out of the way, all that's left is to worry about is the tiny stuff.

Apply the same logic to your time management. "If it's your job to eat a frog, it's best to do it first thing in the morning," Mark Twain famously observed. To put it another way, focus on finishing your most difficult or hated task first thing in the morning. Apart from the fact that we want to get it over with, this is usually when we have the most energy.

16. Switch back and forth between a maker and a manager schedule.

Paul Graham wrote in 2009 that there are two types of schedules: maker's schedules and manager's schedules. A maker's timetable requires you to work alone for hours on the vital tasks. The schedule of a manager is one leader's run-on, full of meetings and check-ins with others.

The notion is intriguing. But, like Malcolm, the majority of us fall somewhere in the middle. That meant there were times when we needed to concentrate on our work without being distracted.

However, there are occasions when we are required to do things such as attend a meeting.

Each is significant in their own right. However, if not properly controlled, it can be disastrous. Let's say you're in the zone when you get a calendar reminder that it's time to walk into the conference room. It's aggravating and inconvenient.

Alternating days is one approach to get around this. Make Mondays a maker's day, for example. Tuesdays, on the other hand, would be manager days because that's when all of your meetings are scheduled.

17. Deal with interruptions on a regular basis.

Like Thanos, interruptions are unavoidable. There are, thankfully, ways for you to triumph over this interplanetary menace to productivity.

Turning off your smartphone notifications is the most obvious place to start. You have the option of turning off your phone, putting it on 'Do Not Disturb,' or blocking apps for a set period of time. Check your notifications at regular intervals to avoid FOMO.

Working in a calm environment is another alternative. IIf this isn't possible, get some noise-cancelling headphones and close the door to your workplace. I'd also recommend posting a sign-up sheet or sharing your calendar with others so that people don't show up unexpectedly.

Also, only accept requests for time that have a reason. Instead of holding a status meeting with your team, utilize project management software to keep track of everyone's progress.

18. Put together your toolkit.

Everyone, whether they own or rent, requires a basic tool kit, which includes screwdrivers, pliers, tape measures, and hammers. Prioritizing your time is the same way. Your productivity toolset should include a planner and a calendar. These are necessary for time management and organization.

You will, however, require equipment to satisfy your specific requirements. Assume you're constructing a home office in your basement. For this project, you'll need sawhorses, circular saws, putty knives, and straight edges.

If you frequently collaborate with people, for example, use AI and machine learning-based project management software and scheduling apps like Calendar. You'll need them to cut down on time spent on time-consuming duties like meeting planning so you can focus on the important stuff.

19. Implement a gamification strategy.

It's all about keeping motivated when it comes to prioritization. And when you're not in the correct frame of mind, it might be difficult. A simple way around this would be to tap into your intrinsic motivation through gamification. For example, break down your goals into micro-goals and reward yourself when you've completed each stage. So, let's say you give yourself an hour to finish writing a report. If you do, then treat yourself to buying those new hiking boots you've been eyeing up.

20. Don't plug leaky boats.

Let's say that you own a small fishing boat. Over time, it begins to leak. That means whenever you go out, you have to either patch it up or constantly bail out water. Not only is this a waste of time, but it's also stressful. Rather than dealing with your battered boat, simply purchase a new one so that you can spend more time doing what you love, which is fishing.

It isn't the objective of this exercise to spend money. It's the notion that anything broken isn't necessarily worth repairing.

21. Make a backwards plan.

"Although extensive research has demonstrated the benefits of planning, little attention has been paid to how people construct plans and their effects on subsequent goal pursuit," said Jooyoung Park, assistant professor in Peking University's HSBC Business School's Department of Management and first author of a paper published in Psychological Science.

When it comes to more difficult activities, his research shows that planning backward is more beneficial. What is the explanation for this? It forces you to anticipate the next step, stay on track with your original plan, and feel less rushed.

22. Keep track of your progress.

When you keep track of your work, you'll be able to see how long each task takes. As a result, you'll be better able to precisely and realistically arrange your time. You can also use this as a guide to identify which jobs can be planned or delegated on a regular basis.

23. Seek out a muse.

Consider some of your favorite musicians. Someone else encouraged them to write and play music. Prioritization works in the same way. Pick the brains of successful and productive people you admire, such as a mentor, a family member, or a well-known company leader. Scout out optimal time prioritizing from someone you respect, whether you're peaking them in person or reading a book they've written.

25. Create your own system for prioritization.

Finally, do what is most comfortable for you. Make your own improvements that match your individual needs, even if you were inspired by someone else. It's similar to being a musician. Because of the blues, a guitar could have picked up the instrument. But, with time, he created his own distinct style that suited his band better.

CHAPTER FIVE

DEALING WITH DISTRACTIONS

Learning to stay focused is a difficult task to achieve. You sit at your desk most days, eager to get some work done. "All right, let's get started," you say to yourself. You open Word or Google Drive and begin working on a fresh document. You have a general concept of what has to be done, but how do you proceed?

You scribble a few words but can't seem to stay focused. "Perhaps I should wake myself up with something fun," you say. You go on Facebook for 20 minutes. Then there's an hour of mindless YouTube video-watching. Lunch will be over before you realize it, and the day will be half through.

You'll get distracted every 11 minutes if you're an average working American, and it'll take you 25 minutes to get back to your task. Furthermore, the more difficult your project is, the longer it will take to refocus. This occurs because moving between complex objectives requires a significant amount of mental work.

Distractions have a significant impact on our ability to focus and be productive. You must learn to deal with distractions in your life if you want to improve or enhance your focus, and here's how.

1. Remind yourself of your vision and objectives

As you learn how to prevent distraction, it's critical to start with a solid foundation for your focus. This entails determining why you require concentration in the first place. Do you have a major presentation at work coming up next week? Do you want to learn to play the guitar but only have an hour per day to practice?

Determining your final aim will assist you in devoting yourself to learning how to focus. Knowing why we need to keep focused will assist us in pushing through the difficult and tiresome aspects of achieving our objectives. That's when our capacity to concentrate is put to the ultimate test, and it's most needed.

2. Before you begin, make sure you have a clear picture of your day.

Spend a few minutes in the morning, before your workday begins,

controlling your schedule. Set your priorities and decide which chores are actually necessary and urgent that day, which are not as urgent but still significant, and which you should avoid, either by delegating or removing them entirely.

This third sort of activity can be challenging since it typically involves urgent but uninspiring topics, such as questions from coworkers about their difficulties, phone calls, and emails that you answer by default because you've always done it and that's how it's always been.

Instead, take command and make a clear decision about what you'll do when they knock. Once you've made it, hold on to it and follow through mercilessly.

3. Make Your Day Less Chaotic

How successful do you think your ability to focus will be if you had 20 chores to complete every day?

If you're too scattered to focus, you won't be able to accomplish those things with sophistication. If you want to learn how to not get sidetracked, you must first break it down to its most basic components.

Limit yourself to only doing two or three essential tasks every day. It includes everything you'll need to get started working toward your goals. Slower is preferable to giving up too soon because you took on too much. In the end, this is healthier for your mental health because you'll be able to watch yourself progressing without becoming easily sidetracked.

4. Complete those tasks as quickly as possible.

To ensure that you complete those 2 to 3 chores, start them early so that you can stay focused on the task without getting overwhelmed. This means you're already planning how to accomplish goals as soon as you wake up.

It's difficult, but putting them off until later will only lead to distraction. Unexpected emails, social media, a child who requires your attention, or coworkers who require assistance with their assignments will all be sources of diversions. All of this might sap your motivation and make it difficult to concentrate on the task at hand.

5. Concentrate on the tiniest aspect of your project at a time.

Seeing a goal as the massive achievement that it is is a simple way to break your concentration. Most goals will take a few weeks to months to complete, and knowing this can make it feel like it will take an eternity.

One of two things will happen as a result:

1. *Because the objective is too lofty, you grow discouraged.*

2. You imagine what it will be like to reach your goal.

Both are bad for your focus and can be an issue when you're trying to focus on the larger picture or using visualization.

Instead, concentrate on doing the bare minimum of work.

If you need to create an article, for example, you know you'll need roughly 1000 words. If that seems overwhelming, try writing 200 words per day for the following five days (or adjust this according to the given deadline). Breaking it down this way will make the process feel more doable and will teach you how to avoid distractions along the way.

6. Create a mental image of yourself at work.

In tip 4, I warned that visualization techniques might occasionally cause more harm than good. There is, however, a legitimate method to use visualization, which is to visualize yourself working.

Champion runners, who normally work backwards, employ this strategy to great effect. They see themselves winning at first, then reverse the process, feeling and visualizing each step all the way back to the start.

Imagine yourself doing a small portion of the task at hand. This is a quicker and more relevant way to apply this.

What should you do, for example, if you need to practice your guitar but it's across the room (let's assume maximum sloth for the sake of this example)?

Consider standing for a moment (really, think of the sensation of getting up, and then do it). It will be simple to act on that feeling if you have truly imagined, pictured, and felt the act of getting up.

Then, with each stage, repeat the vision process until you have the guitar in your hands and are playing it. The practice of concentrating so completely on each step diverts your attention away from how much you don't want to do anything, and the visualizations prepare your body for each step.

All you have to do now is apply this method to whatever it is that you need to concentrate on.

7. Keep Your Internal Distractions Under Control

Internal distractions are one of those things you just can't ignore. You must acquire skills to prepare your mind for work and basic strategies to keep it from wandering to non-essential thoughts in order to learn how to not become distracted.

Internal distractions come in a variety of forms:

Priority Chaos

One of the most prevalent sources of distraction is having too many options available. This may result in a jumbled up priority system.

Some people, for example, may find it difficult to concentrate at home since there are so many possibilities. You have the option of feeding your dog, reading a book, watching TV, eating a snack, or napping.

Aside from the previously indicated distraction costs, priority confusion is a major demotivator. It's difficult to focus your energies and choose one of several potentially appealing possibilities — ideally the one you should be doing.

Priority chaos can also demotivate you by making you feel guilty. You choose to divert your own attention and energy away from your activity when you allow internal distractions to overpower your focus. So you can't blame an external issue if the task you meant to perform doesn't get done. You'll end up criticizing yourself whether you do it deliberately or not!

Why does priority confusion occur? Your brain, on the other hand, prioritizes tasks depending on three factors:

1. *To fill a gap in the market. For example, if you have an urgent need to use the restroom, your brain would undoubtedly prioritize it.*

2. *To achieve a sense of fulfillment, such as that which comes from eating a great chocolate fudge cake.*
3. *The monetary value assigned to achieving the benefit. How much effort, energy, or time will it take to execute this task?*

Even when you're not thinking about it, your brain considers these three factors.

Unfortunately, your brain isn't always the best at making excellent decisions unless you make a conscious effort. It has a proclivity toward short-term benefits and short-term drawbacks.

Because our brains generally associate many more possibilities with short-term rewards, focusing on a work that provides you with a long-term benefit becomes a low priority. Priority Chaos is all about this.

Misalignment of Short and Long-Term Goals

Our brains aren't very excellent at evaluating and comparing short-term and long-term rewards, as previously stated.

Short-term benefits are frequently low-cost and concrete, allowing our brains to comprehend them quickly. Long-term advantages are frequently associated with a large cost, and these perceived costs are rarely as evident. The longer the time horizon, the more difficult it is to envision the rewards. In our brains, this naturally builds a mental barrier and resistance. As a result, we frequently sacrifice long-term profits for short-term profits.

This is why you may know that something is healthy for you in the long run, such as reducing weight and exercising, but you can't seem to get thrilled about it for some reason. You may, on the other hand, be aware that something is harmful to your health, such as binge eating junk food. However, the desire for immediate gratification outweighs your conscious ability to reject it.

This psychological diversion is similar to receiving rapid fulfillment. Thankfully, this may be addressed as well:

1. Determine which work requires the most attention in order to be completed.
2. Break the job down into smaller, more manageable chunks. Each bite-sized activity should have a clear short-term reward (which you can simply articulate in one phrase) and a clear short-term expense (something that you can quantify, such as time spent).
3. Each bite-sized assignment should have a time restriction or duration.
4. The time restriction should be short enough that checking it off becomes a no-brainer.
5. Consider your alternative options. Be true to yourself about what they are. Make a list of all of them, as well as the benefits and expenses connected with each.
6. Start prioritizing your list once you've completed it. You have a limited amount of time, therefore you must prioritize your chores, beginning with the focus task. Then arrange the rest of the items around it.
7. Set aside time for the remaining chores. Don't worry if any of the remaining chores on the list won't fit into your allotted time. You're not obligated to give them up. Simply reschedule them.

8. Eliminate Outside Distractions

This suggestion is a little more basic, as it merely requires you to physically move away from objects that are distracting you.

Turn off the television or work in another room if it is bothering you. If your children are yelling and playing, consider getting up and going to work before they do. If you're always checking your phone, turn it off while you're working. To keep your attention on track, clear the wall in front of you. Your images, prints, and knickknacks are cute, but they'll let your mind wander.

Although it is typically evident what you should do, you should not disregard this piece of advise.

9. Skip What You Don't Understand

This is a suggestion that I have not seen before. If you encounter a drawback in your work, then come back to it later as you learn how to not get distracted. Concentrate your efforts on finding ways to work "mindlessly" at all costs. All this means is that you should start with the simple components.

You may return to the more difficult bits later, and ideally it will have come to you or you will have gained enough momentum that working on it will not break your attention.

10. Focus Practice Will Help You Improve Your Discipline

You can increase your general discipline by doing a few focus exercises.

The first is meditation, which is essentially a practicing definition of focus. It's an excellent way to improve your focus, de-stress, and gain emotional control.

The Pomodoro method, which requires you to set a timer to track how much time you spend on a task, is the second exercise. Each of them is essentially a "concentration sprint," with a solid break in between. You'll become better at them over time, just like you would with actual sprints. Each interval improves your ability to stay focused when it counts, assisting you in learning how to stay focused in the long run.

11. Keep Your Momentum Going

Momentum acts as a lubricant in the discipline process, making it easier to keep to goals. That's why I believe it's critical that we never truly abandon our goals; otherwise, we'll lose momentum and have to rely on discipline to get back on track (not an easy thing to do).

This means we must do something substantial each and every day to advance our objectives (yes, even weekends and holidays). And by "important," I don't necessarily mean a large task, but rather any task that advances us toward our objectives.

If you want to be a freelance writer, for example, compose one solitary pitch over the weekend. Even on Christmas Day, if you want to get healthy, go for a quick 5-minute walk.

Final Thoughts

It's certainly easier said than done to learn how to stay focused. Distractions may be found in almost every aspect of our life these days, even if it's just a little beep from a notification. These types of distractions may appear insignificant, yet anything that takes your attention away from your work can sabotage your productivity.

Make sure you don't get sidetracked. Instead, employ any of the aforementioned strategies to reclaim your focus and overcome distractions. Your productivity will appreciate it.

CHAPTER SIX

No Rush - Slowing Down

Our whole way of life militates against this today. Our civilization has developed a mania for speed, careening out of control in the fast lane of life – a race with no prize and no way of winning.

One sure sign is that no one has enough time. Another is how many of us are always hurrying to be late. Everyone seems to be trying to fit more and more into the same fixed twenty-four hours. That is the paradox: we hurry faster and faster only to find we have less and less time.

Have you noticed that when you try to fit more into a day, you're likely to go through the whole day late? Trying to squeeze more in, we only squeeze time out. Every morning, the first thing we do is look at the *clock; the rest of the day is spent catching up. If we sit down at a table at all, we grab breakfast without actually looking at what's on the table. We seldom notice the food or the faces of individuals we share our lives with.*

And the tempo quickens. We hurry for the bus or fight rush-hour traffic to get to work on time, assuming nothing goes wrong. There isn't even time to smile and say good morning, let alone see who else is in the workplace. They aren't coworkers; they're phantoms obstructing our progress. Of course, they share my sentiments. They have their own to-do list by the end of the day, and only enough time to get it done if they can avoid distractions.

We can't change gears after a day like today. We whirl back home like a boomerang. And we're exhausted by the speed. We take a seat on the bus and close our eyes, and as we do, a mild-mannered gentleman next to us glances up from his paper and innocently says, "What is that three-letter Australian creature with an u at the end of its name?"

We don't want to be obnoxious, but we hear ourselves growl, "Emu!" "I don't care about crossword puzzles!" the mind screams. Who cares about three-letter Australian creatures?" By the time we get home, we're ready to lash out at the first person we meet - who, all too frequently, is someone we care about.

This isn't how we have to live. People who are in charge of their lives manage to arrive on time without being rushed. They get things done without being frazzled about it, but the rest of us, stressed by life's pressures, are constantly a bit late and slightly unprepared as we go from place to place. We've forgotten that it's possible to go about your day without rushing, attending to each issue as it arises without feeling rushed.